SONGS SIGNS AND STORIES

by John Horton

Designed & Illustrated by Michael Kennedy

Teacher's Book Two

ED 11410

Pupil's Edition 11410A

Schott & Co. Ltd, London
48 Great Marlborough Street
London W1V 2BN

B. Schott's Söhne, Mainz

Schott Music Corporation, New York

ED 11410

ISBN 0 901938 66 1

CONTENTS (Book 2)

INDEX OF SONGS (Book 2)

Title or opening words	*Source*	*Teacher's book*	*Pupil's book*
Philadelphia	American	21	18
Quern tune, The	Irish	64	53
Seven hops, The	Dutch	48	40
Since Robin Hood	English	32	27
Tall stories	Spanish	60	50
Ten fingers	Czech	51	42
There was a maid went to the mill	English	70	58
Today the fox will come to town	English	13	11
Twenty, eighteen	English	44	36
Un deux trois	French	50	42
When the miller starts a-milling	Dutch	68	56
When the stormy winds do blow	English	18	15
When the wind comes from the southern side	Dutch	71	59

INDEX OF MELODIES WITHOUT WORDS (Book 2)

ROCKS, STONES AND ECHOES

Stones were not only among man's earliest tools, weapons, and building materials, but also some of his first musical instruments. When chipping, breaking, and shaping stones for his own purposes he heard what seemed like voices coming out of them, and sometimes their shapes reminded him of human beings or animals. In time strange legends grew up around the sounds and shapes of stones.

An ancient Greek story tells how Deucalion escaped, like Noah, from a mighty flood that destroyed all the other inhabitants of his country. With his wife Pyrrha, Deucalion floated in a ship over the flood for five days and nights. When the waters began to go down again the ship rested on Mount Parnassus. Deucalion and Pyrrha prepared thankfully to begin life again on dry land, but they felt lonely with no other human beings around them. They asked the gods for help, and were told that Deucalion must throw 'his mother's bones' over his shoulder. This seemed a strange and disrespectful thing to do, until Deucalion realised that by 'his mother's bones' the gods meant the stones that lay all around on Mother Earth. He and his wife then picked up handfulls of stones and threw them over their shoulders. Those that Deucalion threw turned into men, and those that Pyrrha threw became women, so that the land was soon peopled once more.

Another legend describes how two kings, twin brothers named Zethus and Amphion, ruled over the city of Thebes, and planned to surround it with a strong wall. Zethus was a good workman, and was soon dragging heavy stones into place for his part of the wall. Meanwhile, Amphion seemed to be doing nothing but sitting still and playing quietly on his lyre (a stringed instrument). Zethus began to scoff at his lazy brother, until he realised that the music of Amphion's lyre was causing the stones to move by themselves and take up their positions, so that Amphion's section of the wall was finished first.

A third story is about a wood-nymph named Echo. She was a talkative girl, and so much annoyed Hera, the queen of the gods, with her constant chatter that Hera changed her into a rock. After that poor Echo had to keep silent until someone spoke to her, and even then she could answer only by repeating the last word or two that she heard. Another version of the story says that Echo fell in love with a young man called Narcissus, but he was interested only in gazing at his own reflection in a woodland pool, so that Echo gradually pined away with sorrow until nothing but her voice was left.

Instruments of stone

The simplest way of using stones to make music is to knock them together, as the native musicians of Hawaii do; they use pairs of lava-pebbles, called *ili-ili*. In Ethiopia large slabs of stone are used as church bells. In Vietnam there are complete sets of sounding stones, chipped until they give the right notes, which are laid out on the ground or on a stand and played as if they were xylophones. In ancient China large flat L-shaped stones with a ringing sound were hung on frames and solemnly struck during temple worship or at court ceremonies. The Chinese believed that the voices of the stones could call up the spirits of their ancestors.

One piece of Chinese music is said to be at least three thousand years old. It was played on various instruments, including stone chimes, when the Emperor entered in procession:

(Pupil's 4)

THE EMPEROR'S PROCESSION

Some interesting stone instruments were made in England and can still be seen in museums at Keswick, in Cumbria. They are made from slabs of a particular kind of rock found in the mountain region of Skiddaw. One of the instruments was put together by a stone-mason named Richardson, who worked in the mountains and noticed the musical sound of the stone when he struck it with his hammer. He began to collect suitable slabs and trim them, and after thirteen years he had enough to arrange in rows like the black and white keys of an enormous piano. He and two of his sons then learnt to play pieces of music on the instrument, sitting side by side with a beater in each hand. They gave many concerts, and were invited three times to play to Queen Victoria.

Echoes

We can understand how the legend of Echo grew up. A smooth rock-face or cliff will often throw back any loud sound made near it, and if words are shouted the last word or two will seem to be repeated faintly. The same thing can happen in a cave, a tunnel, or a large building with plenty of empty space, such as a cathedral or covered swimming-bath. We now know that the echo is caused by reflection of the sound, very much as a mirror or pool of water reflects objects near it. Before the scientific explanation was discovered it must have seemed as though someone else was there, repeating the sounds.

It is fun to play echo-games with musical sounds. One singer can echo another, like this:

(Pupil's 6)

Now let the first voice, or 'leader', go straight on without waiting for the echo, so that the two voices overlap. The last bit of echo can go on after the 'leader' has finished, but it makes a more interesting sound if they finish together, holding on to their notes when the 'leader' reaches the end of his scale. This holding-on is marked with a sign called a pause (𝄐). The sounds are held by both partners until one of them gives an agreed signal to stop the singing:

Using echo in this way is really the same thing as singing a round. We have already had several rounds; here is another one, with very suitable words. Two, three, or four voices can take part. The second voice gives the first a bar's start, the third follows after another bar, and so on:

(Pupil's 7)

LOUDLY PLAY AND SWEETLY SING

Sometimes a phrase in a song is repeated like an echo, but without any overlap. This happens with the first and last phrases of each verse of 'Cocky Robin':

COCKY ROBIN

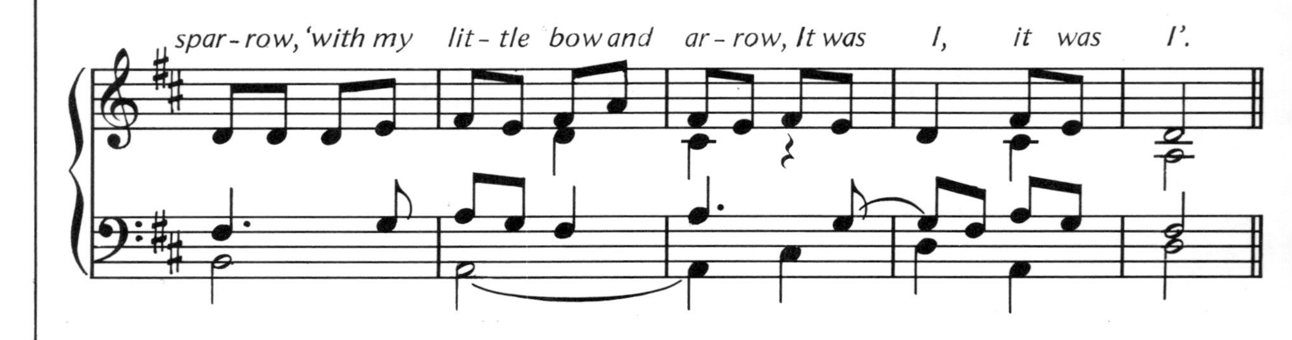

(Pupil's 8)

2 Who saw him die? — Who saw him die? — 'I', said the fly, 'with my
3 Who caught his blood? — Who caught his blood? — 'I', said the fish, 'in my
4 Who made the cof - fin? Who made the cof - fin? 'I', said the crane, 'with my
5 Who dug his grave? — Who dug his grave? — 'I', said the crow, 'with my
6 Who preached the ser - mon? Who preached the ser-mon? 'I', said the swal–low, 'as

(2) lit-tle ti - ny eye. —
(3) lit-tle sil - ver dish. —
(4) lit-tle nar-row plane. —
(5) lit-tle spade and hoe. —
(6) loud as I could hol - loa.

It was I, it was I.'

Things to do

1 If you live near the sea or among mountains you may be able to find stones that give musical sounds when struck. If you cannot get suitable stones, try old roofing tiles, which usually have holes already drilled in them and so can be hung in a row like the Chinese stone chimes.

2 Find out from books on Egypt about the great statues or colossi of Memnon, which 'sang' when the stone was warmed by the morning sun. Find out also about 'singing sands'. These occur in various parts of the world; in Britain some of the best known are at Studland Bay in Dorset, near Nevin in North Wales, and on the island of Eigg in the Hebrides. An explanation of the sound they make when you walk on them is that they are formed of millions of grains of smooth rock. As these rub together they vibrate and each grain makes a tiny squeak.

3 Find out if there are any echoes in places near your home or on your holidays. A famous echo in a building is the Whispering Gallery of St Paul's Cathedral. Another London building that used to have an echo is the Albert Hall. It was difficult to hear music there, because the powerful echo made the sounds of an orchestra overlap so much, but now some devices looking like flying saucers have been hung from the roof, and there is less echo.

(Pupil's 9)

4 If you are interested in science, you can study other kinds of echo, such as:

Living creatures, like bats and dolphins, which are believed to find their way by means of echoes;
Echo-sounding for measuring the depth of the sea and for locating objects like submarines;
Radio echoes, radar, and radio satellite transmission.

5 The story of Deucalion and Pyrrha can be made into a mime with sounds to go with it. The sounds might illustrate:
water the rain splashing, waves rising and sinking, the boat moving on the sea.
wind storm increasing and tossing the boat, then dying down again (voices imitating the noise of the wind).
voices of human beings and of the gods (magnified through cardboard tubes or metal funnels).
stones the rocky landscape, and the throwing of the 'bones' of the earth.

TEACHING NOTES

1 This section opens up a wide range of interrelated studies, from classical myth and legend to modern scientific discoveries and inventions. The former provide scope for creative work combining sound with drama, mime, and other forms of expression.

2 The Deucalion story can be linked with the biblical Noah (and perhaps with the Babylonian legend also). The vivid re-creation of the Noah story in Britten's *Noyes Fludde,* available in recordings, will perhaps be even more enjoyable if the children first try their hands at the Deucalion version.

3 The musical material is on a fairly elementary level, but can be used to revise a number of points of structure and notation and to give further practice in singing and playing in parts.

4 Some reference books:

Percussion Instruments and their History, by James Blades. Faber & Faber, 1970. See the index for references to stone chimes. There are excellent illustrations of the Chinese stone chime *pien-ch'ing*, of other stone instruments (lithophones, pages 90-92) from various places, and of the 'rock harmonicas' of the Keswick district (plates 18-19, descriptions pages 82-84).

Musical Instruments, handbook obtainable from the Horniman Museum, London Road, Forest Hill, London SE23 3PQ.

The Babylonian Legend of the Flood, by Edmond Sollberger. The British Museum, 1971.

Dolphins, by Jacques-Yves Cousteau and Philippe Diolé. Cassell, 1975.

**Tom Brown's School Days*, by Thomas Hughes. The first chapter includes a description of the curious Blowing Stone, in the Vale of White Horse.

THE F SCALE

A scale with F as *doh* fits neatly on to the stave, but to make it work out we have to use a new sign. Suppose we start the F ladder from the top, and go downwards. The four highest steps are easy:

We want a semitone from *doh* to *te*, and we have it, because F—E is one of the 'white semitones' on the piano. The problem comes with the next two steps as we go down, because C—B also is a 'white semitone', and we don't want a semitone in that position. The place where we must have a semitone is at the *next* step, where the sound ought to be *fah-me*. The way we solve the problem is to push that B down and make a new note, called B flat:

(Pupil's 10)

B flat is a black key on the piano, and the xylophone and glockenspiel need extra bars for it. From B flat down to A is only a semitone, so now everything is in order, and we can write the whole scale with both its semitones in their right places:

The flat sign ♭ is really a small letter b with a point at the bottom. B was the first note ever to be flattened in this way, but now the sign is used to make any note a semitone lower.

If we are going to use F as *doh* for any length of time we put a flat on the B line at the beginning. This acts as a key signature, and need only be written once for every line of music.

TODAY THE FOX WILL COME TO TOWN

The word 'town' in this song means somewhere in the country with a farm or a few houses near one another. It is not really a hunting song, but a warning that a fox is on the prowl. Everyone must 'keep' or watch out for him, and drive him off with shouts before he can steal the poultry.

There are two places in the tune where notes are joined together with a curve, like a short slur: These are *tied notes*. The first is three beats long, the second two beats, and they are sung as one long note lasting five beats altogether.

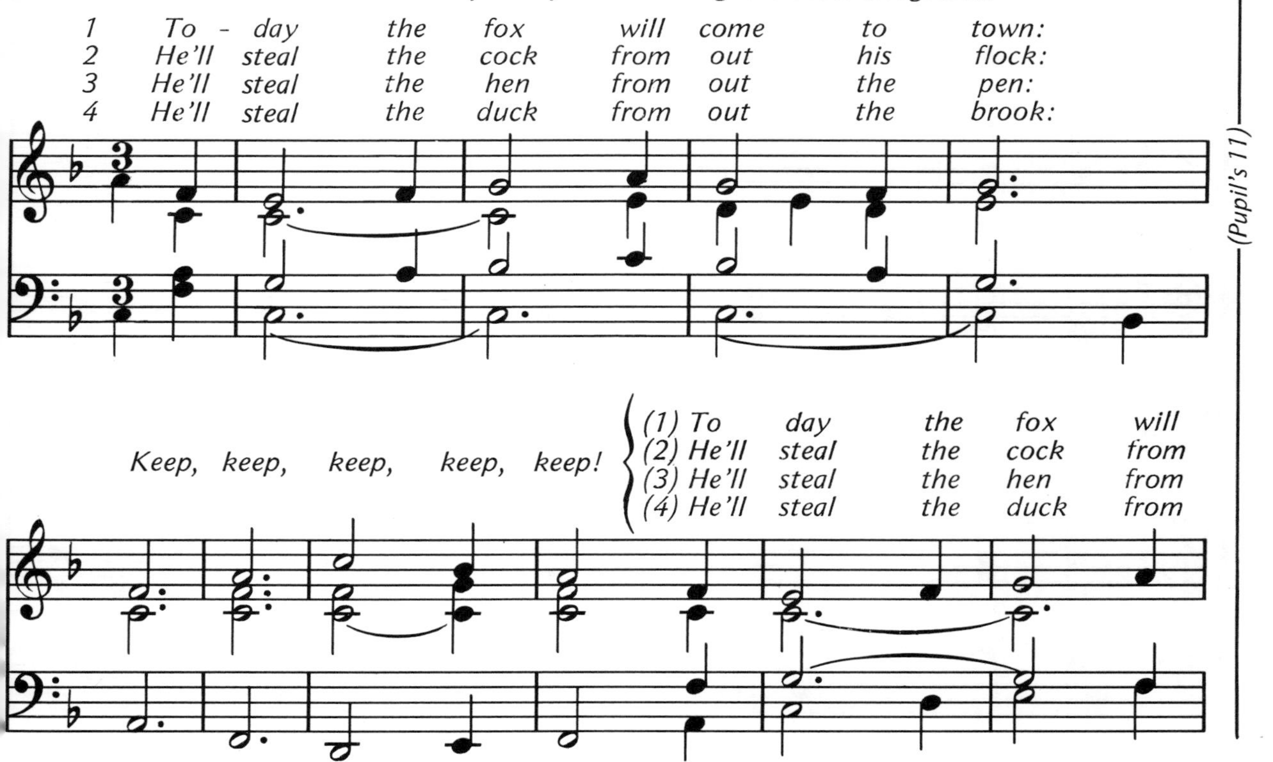

(Pupil's 11)

come to town:
out his flock:
out the pen:
out the brook:
O keep you all well there! I
must de - sire you, neigh - bours all, To hol - loa the
fox from out of the hall, And cry as loud as you can

call: Whoop! whoop! whoop! whoop! whoop! And cry as
loud as you can call: O__ keep you all well there!__

THE MOON

Before trying this Japanese children's song, play an up-and-down ladder on a xylophone, glockenspiel, piano, or recorder:

(Pupil's 13)

Now count how many different letter-names you have played. (The high and low C's of course count as only one letter, and so do the two D's.) Think what notes you would have to put in to make the ladder into an ordinary F scale.

This is a scale with no semitones – no *me-fah* (A-B flat) or *te-doh* (E-F). We call it a *pentatonic scale,* and we often hear it in music from lands in the far east, like Japan and China. The whole song is made out of these five sounds, and so is the companion tune (marked *Instruments*) which can be played as an accompaniment.

looks at me! She's ne-ver ol-der that I can see.
looks at me! Great sun's sis-ter she sure-ly must be.
She grows round, it is quite true; some-times she is
Mir-ror - round, and some-times, too, like a comb of
ve - ry new. Spring and sum - mer, au-tumn and
sil - ver curled. Spring and sum - mer, au-tumn and

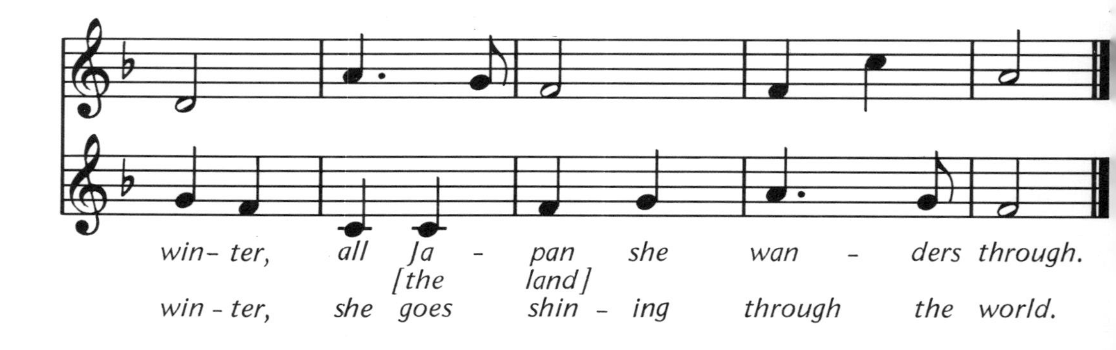

WHEN THE STORMY WINDS DO BLOW

(Pupil's 15)

This fine old song about the life of a sailor belongs to the days when British sailing-ships and British seamen were becoming known all over the world. It can still mean a great deal to us in modern times if we remember the perils and excitements of the fishing fleets, the North Sea oil rigs, and lonely voyages in sailing craft.

(1) ease, How lit – tle do you think u – pon the dan-gers of the
(2) shun; In eve – ry kind of wea - ther still his course he has to
(3) shore, The hor - rors of the tem - pest now we think up – on no
(1) seas; Give ear un-to the ma – ri-ners, and they will plain-ly
(2) run; Now moun - ted on the top-mast high, how fear - ful 'tis be-
(3) more. We find a hear - ty wel - come there, wher – e – ver we may
(1) show All_ the cares and_ the fears when the stor-my winds do blow.
(2) -low; Then_we ride with_ the tide when the stor-my winds do blow.
(3) go; Safe_and sound on_ dry ground when the stor-my winds do blow.

Things to do

(Pupil's 16/17)

1 Practise making the flat sign, putting it on the *middle* line of the stave so that the line shows through the sign:

With this key signature we know that F is *doh*, B flat is *fah*, and D is *lah*.

2 Fit out a glockenspiel, xylophone, or set of chime bars with the five notes C, D, E, G, A, and an extra C and D at the top:

From this scale, which is pentatonic (only 5 *different* note-names), you can make up tunes that suggest the music of far-eastern lands. Here are the beginnings of two melodies some of the first European travellers to China heard there and tried to write down. Later they brought them back to Europe, where some famous composers borrowed them to use in their own music:

3 An easy way of finding a ready-made pentatonic scale is to play on the five different black keys of the piano, without touching any of the white ones.

4 Here are two old American songs from the mountains of Kentucky. Work out the letter names of their five different notes, and then practise singing and playing them:

OLD BALD EAGLE

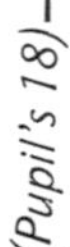

TEACHING NOTES

1 The useful F scale, involving the introduction of the flat sign, should give few notational problems. It is not, however, the happiest of keys for recorders, and if these instruments are used special attention will be needed for the rather awkwardly-fingered F and lower C, as well as for the unfamiliar B flat.

2 The three songs differ widely in character and standard of difficulty, and it is not expected that all three will appeal to the same age-groups. The Japanese song, with its English version by Grace Hazard Conkling, is for the younger ones, though older people could gain something from examining its pentatonic structure and attempting the instrumental counter-melody. The B flat key signature is of course not strictly necessary, but has been given for the sake of uniformity.

3 Of the Chinese tunes whose beginnings are quoted in C pentatonic, tune *A* is a form of the one used by Puccini in his last opera, *Turandot*, where it is first heard sung off-stage by a children's choir. Tune *B* was borrowed from Weber's stage music to *Turandot* (a play by Gozzi, translated by Schiller) as one of the themes for Hindemith's *Symphonic Metamorphoses*. The Chinese melody is treated there in variation form with brilliant orchestration, including a large percussion section; this would make a good piece for children to enjoy from a recording.

4 'Today the fox will come to town' ('today' substituted for the traditional 'tomorrow' to avoid rhythmic complications) is sung to the dance tune *Trenchmore*, which as we shall note later was in the repertory of Elizabethan dancers and musicians. It is important in teaching this song to catch the lilt of the dance, and especially to avoid too slow a tempo. The notation usually given is in $\frac{6}{4}$ time, but a moderate $\frac{6}{8}$ (i.e. 2 ♩.) would be even more appropriate.

5 The robust sea song 'When the stormy winds do blow' gets much of its vigour from the recurrent time pattern ♩. ♪ . In this song also the tempo should be quite brisk.

6 The two little pentatonic songs given under 'Things to do' were collected by Cecil Sharp from a Kentucky singer, Mr Hillard Smith, on 20 September 1917. No other words were recorded.

THE GUARDIAN OF THE WINDS

Among the many adventures that befell the warrior Odysseus and his men on their voyage home after the siege of Troy was their meeting with the Guardian of the Winds. They landed on a floating island with a great wall of bronze around it. The ruler of this island was named Aeolus, and the gods had entrusted to him all the winds that blow. Aeolus treated the wanderers kindly, and with his large family of sons and daughters, entertained them royally for a whole month. When they were ready to leave, the king put into the hold of Odysseus' ship a leather bag fastened with a silver clasp. In this bag Aeolus had shut up all the winds except a gentle western breeze which would waft the ship homewards to the island of Ithaca.

They sailed on peacefully, with all sails set, for nine days and nights, until they could see the shores of Ithaca. Soon they were so close that they could make out the wisps of wood-smoke rising from the house-tops, and Odysseus lay down contentedly to sleep on deck. But while he rested, the crew began to murmur among themselves. That leather bag in the hold, they said, must surely contain gold and silver, and they wanted their share, as they had been with their master through all his wanderings and hardships.

At last they agreed to unfasten the silver clasp and find what was inside. The moment they did so, all the winds rushed out together, the waves rose high around them, the ship was blown back and forth, and they were rapidly carried out to the open sea and back to the island kingdom of Aeolus. The Guardian of the Winds was astonished to see them, for he thought he had done all he could to bring them safely home. Odysseus tried to explain how his crew had opened the bag while he slept, and he begged Aeolus to forgive them and help them again.

(Pupil's 19)

But Aeolus was both angry and afraid. Odysseus, he said, must have offended the gods in some way to bring this misfortune on his head, and it would be dangerous to help such an unlucky man.

There was nothing for it but to set out once more. This time there was no gentle wind to waft them, but only a dead calm, and the crew had to toil night and day at the oars. After six days' hard rowing they reached unknown land where they hoped to find food, water, and shelter. But it was inhabited by cannibal giants who hurled rocks at the ships to sink them, and then carried off the drowning men to devour them. Only Odysseus and a few of his men escaped, and they had to go through more perils and sufferings until Odysseus, alone of all his crew, drifted on to the shore of Ithaca.

Things to do

1 Read more of the adventures of Odysseus (or Ulysses).

2 See how many words you can find to describe the movement and sound of gentle and strong winds.

3 Find out how the strength of winds is measured on the Beaufort scale.

4 Collect sayings and rhymes connected with the wind. Here is one to start with:

When the wind is in the north
the skilful fisher goes not forth.
When the wind is in the south
it blows the bait in the fish's mouth.
When the wind is in the east
it's good for neither man nor beast.
When the wind is in the west
it's then it's at its very best.

5 Find out about a strange musical instrument named after the Guardian of the Winds. It is called the Aeolian harp, and is made by stretching strings or thin wires across a frame and fixing it in an open window, so that the wind can blow upon the strings. There is no tune, but a mysterious humming as several strings vibrate at the same time.

(Pupil's 20)

(Pupil's 21/22)

It is something like the sound made by telegraph wires or overhead electric cables when a strong wind makes them vibrate.

6 Try some of the experiments that follow, to discover how air vibrates and makes musical sounds.

1 Pull out the handle of a bicycle pump as far as it will go, put your thumb firmly over the valve hole so that no more air can enter or escape, and push the handle back as hard as you can. Then release the handle, making sure that the valve hole is still firmly covered. What do you notice? What do you think this experiment shows about air?

2 Blow across the end of a cardboard tube, and listen to the sound it makes. Do the same thing again, but this time cover the bottom end of the tube firmly with the palm of your hand. What difference have you made to the sound?

3 Blow across the ends of plastic straws (or real straws if you can get them: oaten ones are best) until you get a clear sound. Then try cutting the straw to shorten it, and notice how the sound changes.

4 Blow across the open end of a milk or mineral water bottle and listen to the sound. Then pour a few inches of water into the bottle and notice how the sound changes. Try this with different amounts of water.

5 Take several bottles of the same size, arrange them in a row, and check that they all make the same kind of sound when you blow across them. Then pour a different amount of water into each bottle until you have a scale. As a change from blowing, try tapping gently on the top rim of the bottle with a wooden kitchen spoon.
Warning: if you tap the *sides* of the bottles, or use glass tumblers instead, you will spoil the experiment, because you have turned the glass into a kind of bell, which obeys different laws.

6 Take off the top joint of your recorder and blow gently into it. Then put it back into its place, use the fingers of both hands

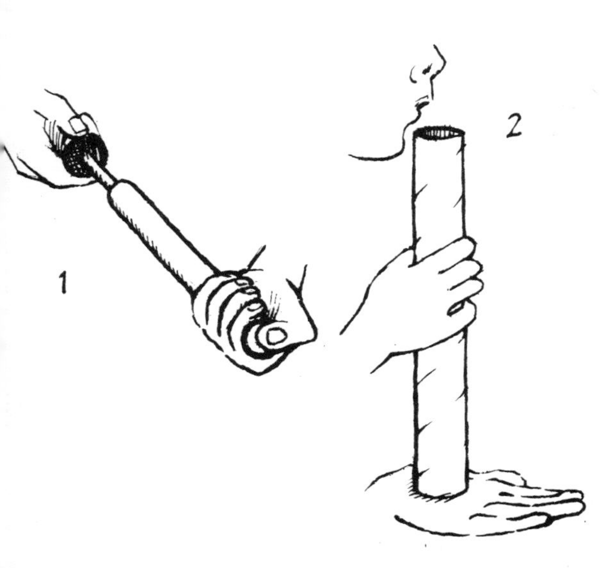

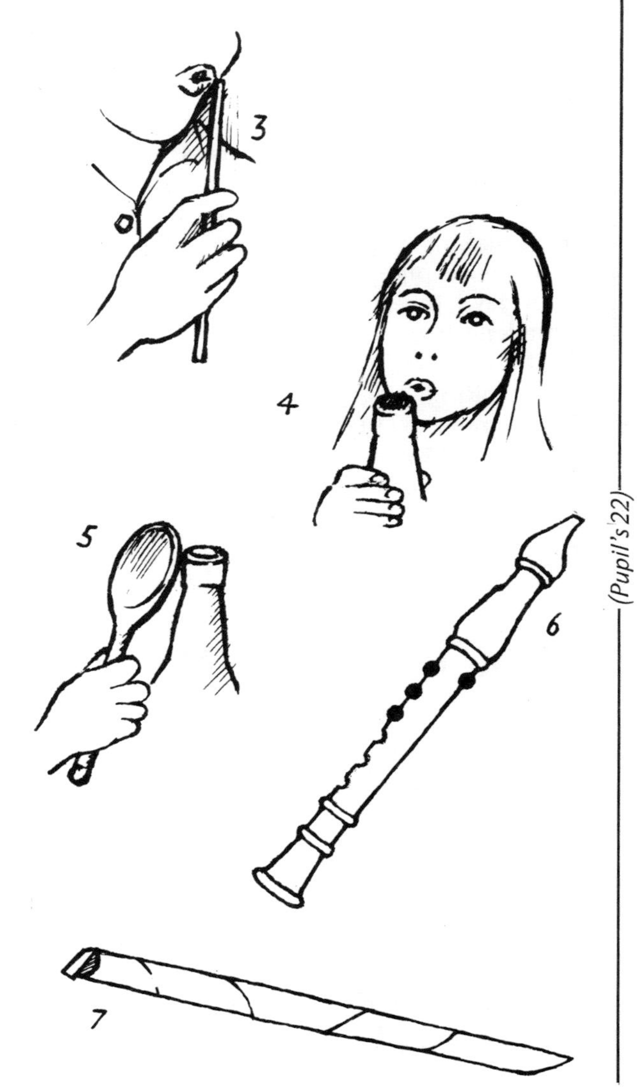

to cover all the holes of the recorder, and blow again. Now take your right-hand fingers away and listen to the sound when only the left-hand holes are covered.

7 Make a buzzer by rolling a square of thin but strong paper diagonally round a pencil. Fix the roll with a bit of sellotape and slip the pencil out. You will now have a pipe with a small triangle at each end. Cut one of the triangles very carefully so that you can fold it like a flap over the end of the pipe. It must fit close, but be free to move up and down. Put the flap end into your mouth, close your lips but not your teeth, and blow gently. The flap should begin to vibrate and the pipe will make a buzz. (Don't be discouraged if this does not work at first. It helps if the flap is moistened slightly.)

(Pupil's 22)

What we have learnt from the experiments

1 Air is springy or 'elastic'. Although it is invisible, it can be squeezed like rubber and bounces back again.
2 The air in a tube can be made to vibrate in several ways: by blowing across one end, by blowing through a narrow opening on to a sharp edge in the 'window' of the recorder, or by making a tongue or 'reed' vibrate.
3 A closed pipe, blocked at one end, sounds an octave lower than an open pipe of the same length.
4 The shorter we make the column of air or 'speaking length', the higher the sound.
5 The more air there is to vibrate in a narrow bottle, the lower the sound. Adding water fills up some of the air space.

(Pupil's 23)

TEACHING NOTES

1 Books of simplified stories from Homer's *Odyssey* are plentiful, and there is an excellent complete translation of the entire work, made by E. V. Rieu and published in Penguin Classics. The Aeolus episode comes at the beginning of Book 10.

2 The Aeolian harp is described and pictured in Scholes's *Oxford Companion to Music* and other works of reference; *Science and Music* by Sir James Jeans, Cambridge University Press, 1937, pages 128-9, gives a scientific explanation of its working.

3 Other ancient legends and myths are connected with wind instruments: for example, the story of Pan and Syrinx.

4 Interesting facts about air and its movements are given in simple language and with attractive illustrations and diagrams in *The Weather*, by F. E. Newing and Richard Bowood (A Ladybird Book). The Ladybird Leader book **Sounds* has already been recommended; another useful title in that series is **Musical Instruments* by Ann Rees, illustrated by Robert Ayton.

5 The elementary experiments given above are capable of much extension, both scientific and musical, including their application to orchestral wind instruments and to the pipe organ. A handy reference book for the teacher is the Pelican *Musical Instruments through the Ages*, edited by Anthony Baines.

WILL KEMP'S DANCE FROM LONDON TO NORWICH

William Kemp lived in the reign of the first Queen Elizabeth. He was the clown or comic actor in some of Shakespeare's plays, and could make the audience laugh the moment he came on to the stage. He was also a fine and athletic dancer. Besides dancing in the theatre as part of his act, he undertook long-distance dances, earning both fame and money from wealthy people who sponsored him and from the crowds that gathered along the roadside to watch him. He was famous not only in England, but also abroad in Germany, France and Italy. His greatest feat of endurance was to dance the morris, a lively and strenuous dance popular at that time, all the way from the City of London to Norwich. It took him nine days altogether, not counting the time for resting, meals, and sleep. He wrote an account of his journey in a little book called *Kemp's Nine Days' Wonder*, with a picture of himself in embroidered jacket, wide breeches, a hat with a large feather, scarves hanging from his arms, and bunches of little bells tied to his legs. Beside him in the picture marches his companion, Thomas Slye, playing music for the morris dance on a three-holed pipe and a tabor or small drum.

Here is a diary of Kemp's dance from London to Norwich:

First day He started at seven in the morning one fine Monday in early spring from the Lord Mayor's House in the City of London. Three men were with him – Thomas Slye with his pipe and tabor, George Sprat who acted as 'overseer' or referee to see that Kemp took no extra rests, and a manservant, William Bee. Hundreds of people had turned out to see them start, and many of them threw money to encourage them. Kemp danced along Whitechapel to Stratford, Mile End, and Ilford, where he politely refused a drink out of the Great Spoon of Ilford which held a quart of liquor. At Romford he spent two days resting at an inn; he was glad enough to have got there

(Pupil's 24)

in safety, as just outside the town he was nearly trampled under the hooves of a pair of runaway horses.

Second day Thursday began badly, for Kemp strained a muscle, but cured it simply by going on dancing, and so got to Brentwood, where it was market day. The streets were crowded, and two men were caught picking pockets. They pretended they were officially collecting for Kemp's dance, but when Kemp assured the authorities that he had never set eyes on the rogues before they were punished and sent back to London, where they had come from. Kemp then danced on to Ingatestone. It was now night-time, but about fifty people still followed him by moonlight.

Third day (Friday) The crowd had grown to about two hundred as Kemp set out in the morning for the large town of Chelmsford. It took him more than an hour to push his way through the people and to reach his inn, and by that time he felt so exhausted that he could not dance another step. So he spoke to the waiting crowds from his bedroom window, and explained that being in training he could not accept any of their invitations to dinner. But he soon began to get over his weariness, and kindly allowed a girl of fourteen, who seems to have been the local junior champion, to dance the morris with him in the largest room of the inn. She managed to keep up with him for a whole hour, until Kemp was obliged to confess that the strongest man in Chelmsford could not have done so well. He took a weekend rest until Monday.

(Pupil's 25)

Fourth day The way from Chelmsford to Braintree was long and muddy, with thick woods on both sides and deep holes in the road. Two country lads tried to join in Kemp's dance, one of them just ahead of him and the other at his heels. At last they came to a puddle so wide that Kemp had to take a flying leap at it, reaching the other side up to the ankles in dirty water. One of the youths trying to follow him fell right in the middle of the pool and had to be rescued by the other. After that they left Kemp to go on by himself to Braintree, where he rested for two nights.

Fifth day Wednesday's stretch took him to Sudbury, in Suffolk. A burly man, a butcher by trade, offered to keep him company as far as Bury St Edmunds, but after only half a mile he also dropped out, saying he could not keep up if he were offered a hundred pounds. Another young girl appeared, however, borrowed some of Kemp's bells to tie on her legs, and actually stayed the course as far as Long Melford. There Kemp was met by a gentleman named Mr Coles, who took him to his house and entertained him from Wednesday night until Saturday morning.

Sixth day Mr Coles's household jester danced along with Kemp for part of the way from Long Melford to Clare, and later a wealthy widow invited Kemp to her home and gave him a splendid meal. At last he reached the great town of Bury St Edmunds in the afternoon. At that very moment the Lord Chief Justice of England happened to be entering the town through another gate, but Kemp was proud to find that it was his dancing, and not the Chief Justice's procession, that attracted the largest crowds. Unfortunately the weather changed, and Kemp had to stay snowed up in Bury until the following Friday morning.

Seventh day This was Friday in the third week of Kemp's journey. By now the snow was thawing, and he made good progress from Bury across the heath (now called the Breckland) to Thetford, covering the ten miles in three hours. As it was assize time, Thetford was more crowded than usual, but a gentleman named Rich was true to his name, let Kemp stay in his fine house for two days, and then sent him on his way with a gift of five pounds.

Eighth day (Monday) The next stop was an inn at Rockland. The innkeeper was so proud of having a famous visitor like Kemp that he put on his best suit of clothes and began to make a speech in his honour. But the poor man was overcome with nervousness, and all he could stammer out was: 'Master Kemp, you are as welcome as — as the Queen's best greyhound'. The innkeeper even tried to accompany his guest as far as Hingham, but was much too fat to keep up with the dance. The local youths and girls kept offering to show Kemp the easiest way through the slushy lanes.

Ninth day Now came the last stage of the journey. From Hingham, by way of Barford Bridge, Kemp arrived at the city of Norwich. But it was hopeless to try and dance through the crowd that thronged the streets, and Kemp decided to ride in on a borrowed horse, though he knew that to keep the rules made for him he would have to do the morris through the streets later on.

So he rode into the market place, where the city musicians or 'waits' were all ready, wearing their silver-gilt chains and holding their instruments with red and white silk banners attached, to play in Kemp's honour as they had played for the Queen herself a few years earlier. Kemp thought these Norwich musicians were as good as any in the country, and later wrote in his book:

> *'Besides their excellence in wind instruments, their rare cunning on the viol and violin, their voices are admirable, every one of them able to serve in any cathedral church as choristers.'*

Will Kemp knew that the Mayor and Corporation were waiting in the Guildhall, dressed in their furred robes, to give him a civic welcome, but the crowd pressed so closely round him that the horse could not move. So he jumped off its back, skipped over a low church wall, and found another way into the Guildhall. In the meantime the 'overseer', George Sprat, had completely lost sight of Kemp among the crowd, and insisted that the last bit of the journey would have to be done all over again. But by this time the Mayor and Corporation were receiving Kemp with every honour Norwich citizens could offer him. He was given five pounds in gold on the spot, and a pension of forty shillings a year for life; he was made a

(Pupil's 26)

Freeman of the Merchant Venturers' Company; and the boots in which he had come all the way from London were solemnly hung on the walls of the Guildhall. And so ended Kemp's Nine Days' Wonder.

Will Kemp's Music The three-holed pipe to which Kemp danced was something like a small recorder, but much harder to play, as all the notes of the tunes had to be made with the first two fingers and thumb of the left hand, while the other left-hand fingers held the pipe between them and the right hand beat the tabor to mark the time. Kemp knew how to play the pipe and tabor himself, but when dancing he had to leave it to Thomas Slye. We do not know what morris tunes Slye chose to play on the famous nine days' journey, but we can make a good guess at some of them. We know that Kemp was fond of the tune called 'Trenchmore', which is the one we have already sung to the words 'Today the fox will come to town'. The tune on this page has words mentioning Kemp and some of the usual figures in the morris when it is danced by a team:

(Pupil's 27)

SINCE ROBIN HOOD

Another tune, called 'Watkin's Ale', also has words that refer to Kemp's exploits abroad. The words stop after the first eight bars, but we have printed the whole tune, which is quite long, so that you can play all of it if you like.

WATKIN'S ALE

Last of all, here is a tune known as Kemp's Jig. There are a few signs in it that we have not come across before. The empty-headed note without a stem **o** is a *semibreve*, and must be held for four whole beats. The tune is in the G scale, and therefore has an F sharp key signature, making nearly all the F's into F sharps. But in two places the F sharp is 'cancelled' by means of a sign called a *natural* (♮). In those places we play F and not F sharp. Soon afterwards the sharp is put back again. Then, just once, there is a B flat. Notes which do not really belong to the key we are using, but crop up occasionally, are called *chromatic notes*. These particular ones, F sharp and B flat, are quite easy to play on the recorder.

(Pupil's 30)

KEMP'S JIG

(Pupil's 32)

The Betley Window

Reproduced by permission of Lord Bridgeman

Things to do

1 Make a map of Kemp's journey from London to Norwich, and find the distances between some of the places mentioned in the story. A motoring road book will help; the roads do not run quite the same as they did in the time of Elizabeth I, but Kemp's route was roughly along the present A11, A118, A12, A131 and A134.

2 Find out more about the old town musicians or 'waits'. Those of Norwich who played to Kemp were so famous that in 1589 Francis Drake borrowed six of them to take in his ship when he went to Corunna to 'singe the King of Spain's beard' (meaning to set his fleet on fire). A few years earlier another Elizabethan seaman, Sir Humphrey Gilbert, had not only musicians but also morris dancers in his ships when he sailed to Newfoundland to plant an English settlement. The morris dancers were to entertain the sailors and to please the native people and make them more friendly.

3 Learn how to dance some of the morris steps. As we have seen, the dance can be done by one or two persons, but a full team or 'side' was made up of at least eight dancers, some of them dressed to represent different characters. If you examine the picture on page 38 you will see the characters in a full team. This picture shows an old stained glass window in Staffordshire. See if you can find the hobby horse, the fool or jester, the pipe and tabor player, the man dressed as Maid Marian, the Friar, and some dancers with bells on their legs.

(Pupil's 33)

TEACHING NOTES

1 *Kemp's Nine Days' Wonder* is reprinted in full in A. C. Ward's *Tracts and Pamphlets*, World's Classics, Oxford University Press, 1927. The whole story is rich in historical and geographical material, as well as in music and folklore.

2 A description of the pipe and tabor, and the technique of playing, will be found in *The Instruments of Music* by Robert Donington, University Paperbacks, page 98.

3 Instructions for the morris dance, and further information on the history and background of the dance, can be obtained from the English Folk Dance and Song Society, Cecil Sharp House, London NW I.

4 The second and third tunes given in the pupils' books are woven together in Thomas Weelkes's madrigal, 'Since Robin Hood': see *The Music Group*, Book 5, Edition Schott 11132. 'Watkin's Ale' appears in the Fitzwilliam Virginal Book in an anonymous setting; the other tune ('Since Robin Hood' . . .) is of course the same as the traditional Helston Furry Dance. 'Kemp's Jig' is taken from *English Lute Music* (16th century), transcribed by David Lumsden, Edition Schott 10311, page 54; a few alterations have been made to bring the tune within the compass of the descant recorder.

5 A full description of the remarkable Betley Window will be found in the *Journal of the English Folk Dance and Song Society*, Volume VII, no. 2. It is by Mr. E. J. Nicol, through whose courtesy and that of the owner of the window, Lord Bridgeman, the photograph is reproduced here.

6 Drake's application for the services of the Norwich waits is minuted in the records of the City of Norwich for 25 January 1589. The City agreed to pay for six new cloaks for the waits, and to grant £4 to buy three new hautboys and a treble recorder, 10 shillings for a sackbut case, £10 for general expenses, and the cost of a wagon to transport the waits to Drake's embarkation point.

The report of Sir Humphrey Gilbert's preparations, included in *Richard Hakluyt Voyages and Documents*, edited by Janet Hampden, World's Classics, page 250, reads:

'We were in number in all about 260 men, among whom we had of every faculty good choice, as Shipwrights, Masons, Carpenters, Smiths, and such like . . . Besides, for solace of our people and allurement of the Savages, we were provided of Music in good variety, not omitting morris dancers, hobby horses, and May-like conceits to delight the savage people, whom we intended to win by all fair means possible.'

7 Over Easter 1977, during the twenty-fifth year of the reign of Queen Elizabeth II, more than twenty morris teams danced in relays as far as possible over the route Will Kemp had taken nearly four centuries earlier, in the reign of Elizabeth I. They wore traditional morris dress, and their musical instruments included mouth organ, violin, accordion, and tabor. The first team started from the Guildhall, with a send-off from the Lord Mayor of London, and four days later 'Kemp's Men of Norwich', who formed the final relay, were welcomed officially in their own city.

COUNTING AND NUMBERING

Numbers and figures have a great deal to do with helping us to understand how music is made and how it is written down.

1 Every musical sound has its *frequency* or vibration-number: for example, the note A

is made by a string vibrating nearly 440 times in a second. A string that vibrated twice as fast (880 times a second) would sound an octave higher

2 If we want to know how fast to play a piece of music, we sometimes use a metronome to help us. We set the metronome so that it ticks so many times in a minute; for example, if we set it to the figure 60 it will tick that number of times per minute, or once a second. Crotchets played at that speed (♩ = 60) will be quite slow. ♩ = 120 would mean two crotchet beats a second, or twice as fast.

3 We also count to make sure how long a sound has to last, and we can put these different lengths into a kind of multiplication table:

1 crotchet beat ♩

2 crotchets make 1 minim 𝅗𝅥

3 crotchets make 1 dotted minim 𝅗𝅥.

4 crotchets make 1 semibreve 𝅝

We use fractions, too:

half a crotchet beat is 1 quaver ♪

a whole crotchet equals 2 quavers ♫

one dotted crotchet ♩. plus one quaver ♪ makes up 2 whole beats (1½ + ½).
Quarter beats are shown by 4 semiquavers

4 Another use for counting is to find how many bars make up a phrase, and how many phrases a complete tune contains.

5 Then there are the time-signatures, which remind us how the beats are grouped — in twos: 2 or threes: 3 or fours: 4 .
(Another way of writing these is $\frac{2}{4}$, $\frac{3}{4}$, $\frac{4}{4}$ or **C**).

6 Another important use for counting is to be able to say how far one sound is higher or lower than the next, or what *interval* they are apart. You can remember the names of the intervals if you learn this amusing little song:

(Pupil's 34)

(Pupil's 35)

7 We use numbers to show fingering. In piano playing the thumbs count as 1 and the other fingers as 2, 3, 4, 5, ending with the little finger. With some other instruments, like the violin, which do not use the thumbs to make sounds, the numbering starts with the index finger and goes 1, 2, 3, 4.

Songs with counting words **Most people know a few songs of this kind, such as 'One man went to mow' and 'The animals went in two by two'. Here are some more:**

TWENTY, EIGHTEEN

In this we have to count *backwards*, **first in even numbers and then in odd numbers. Some of the old country singers liked to have a competition over it, to see who could sing the counting words fastest without making a slip.**

(1) Till she do say 'yes' or 'no.'
(2) I may come this way a-gain.
(3) All shall be at your command.
(4) All I want's a handsome man.
Twen-ty, eigh-teen, six-teen, four-teen,
twelve, ten, eight, six, four, two, none;
nine - teen, seven - teen,
fif - teen, thir - teen, e - le-ven, nine, seven, five, three and one.

THE DILLY SONG

The counting here is easier, but the words are full of mystery and no one understands exactly what they mean, though they seem to have a great deal to do with ancient legends and religious beliefs. Every verse begins with two questions and two answers, so that it is a good idea to share the song between two people or two groups of singers.

1 One of them is all a-lone, and e – ver will re – main so.
2 Two of them are lily-white ba - bies dres-séd all in green O!
3 Three of them are strangers, o'er the wide world they are ran – gers.
4 Four it is the Dil-ly Hour, when blooms the gil - ly - flow – er.
5 Five it is the Dil-ly Bird, that's ne – ver seen but heard O!
6 Six the Ferryman in the boat, that on the ri - ver floats O!
7 Seven it is the Crown of Heaven, the shin-ing stars be seven O!
8 Eight it is the morning break, when all the world's a – wake O!
9 Nine it is the pale moonshine, thepalemoonshine is nine O!
10 Ten forbids all kind of sin, and then be - gins a – gain O!
[Varied accompaniments]

THE SEVEN HOPS

This Dutch song needs not only counting and singing, but also action. At the word *one* you put your left foot forward, at *two* your right foot; at *three* you put the left foot forward again and bend that knee, at *four* right foot forward and bend that knee; at *five* put your left elbow on the floor, at *six* your right elbow; and at *seven* try to touch the floor with your nose. If you like you can then repeat the song with all the movements in reverse until you are standing straight up again.

(Pupil's 40)

dance like a - ny no- ble-man. That is one! That is two! That is
three! That is four! That is five! That is six! That is se - ven!

(Pupil's 41)

UN DEUX TROIS

If you know some French, this song will give you practice in counting up to 12. The word *neuf* means 'nine' the first time it comes, but the second time it has its other meaning 'new' (so that *dans mon panier neuf* means *in my new basket*).

(Pupil's 42)

TEN FINGERS

This is a very easy little song for counting on all the fingers. It is printed here in a scale we have not used before, with A as *doh.* If you experiment, you find that *three* sharps are necessary for this scale — the F sharp and C sharp we have used already, and a new note, G sharp, to make the semitone just below A. In the key signature this G sharp is hoisted into the space right on top of the stave.

Things to do

1 On page 42 are the vibration-rates or frequencies of two of the A's on the piano. See how many other A's you can find on the keyboard, and then work out their frequencies.

2 Find out something about the inventor Mälzel (or Maelzel), who gave his name to the clockwork metronome.

3 Look carefully through the song 'Twenty, Eighteen', and find all these intervals somewhere or other in the tune:

a *second*
a *third*
a *fourth*
a *fifth*
a *seventh*

4 The two notes of an interval need not always come one after the other. They can be sung or played so that they sound together. Here is a set of intervals made out of the F scale. Try playing them with a pair of beaters on a glockenspiel or xylophone, or with two forefingers on the piano. Start with both beaters or both fingers on the same note (this is called a *unison*), and gradually widen the interval until you reach the *octave*. Don't forget the B flat.

5 When you have found all the intervals, and can play them while counting two beats to each, get a descant recorder player to fit the first two phrases of 'Twenty, Eighteen' on top of your intervals; or you can make a piano duet of it, like this:

(Pupil's 44)

TEACHING NOTES

1 The connections between music and numbers are endless, and only a few of the simplest are dealt with in this section. The educationists of the Middle Ages included Music in the *Quadrivium* along with other non-verbal studies – Arithmetic, Geometry, and Astronomy, and although their outlook was mainly speculative and theoretical, the practical bearings of mathematics on musical construction and performance cannot be ignored even in the most elementary musical work. An interesting and stimulating book (for the teacher) is *The New Soundscape*, by the Canadian composer and teacher R. Murray Schafer (published in 1969 by BMI Canada Limited).

2 The section contains some elementary study of intervals, on which later skills in melodic and chordal analysis can be built if required. At this stage nothing is said about the *quality* of intervals, though some of the abler children might be encouraged to discover, with the aid of the keyboard, that some diatonic seconds contain one semitone, others two; that some thirds are 'minor', with a tone and a half, and others 'major', with two whole tones. On the other hand, most pupils may need help in grasping the basic fact that an interval is named according to the number of letter-names it covers.

3 Why do all A's sound similar, all B's, all C's and so on? The acoustical explanation is worth giving, especially if it is accompanied by some practical experiments with stretched strings, dividing them into halves, quarters etc. If a set of recorders is available, the descant instrument might be compared with the tenor, the treble with the bass.

4. 'Twenty, Eighteen', collected around the beginning of the present century from a Norfolk singer named John Graham, is a version of the better-known 'Keys of Canterbury' and 'Keys of Heaven' with the addition of the forfeit numbering refrain. 'The Dilly Song' also exists in a great many versions in half a dozen languages. Learned explanations of the words are often attempted, but the very obscurity of the allusions may give them a special appeal to young children. The amusing Dutch singing-game is a trial of both memory and physical agility. The French nursery song about cherry-picking has been printed with the number-words in full, as they are normally pronounced in everyday speech, rather than with elision-marks that might baffle a beginner in the language. The ten-finger rhyme is based on a Moravian children's song.

5 The A major key signature is introduced at this point, as it will soon be needed fairly often. The G sharp, however, does not occur in the Moravian nursery song.

6 Among relevant opera recordings that might be used in connection with some of the topics in this section are the opening of Ravel's *L'Heure espagnole* (the clockmaker's shop, with clocks and watches of all sizes ticking and striking against one another — a marvellous mathematical-musical sound), the spine-chilling scene in Wolf's Glen, with the casting of magic bullets by numbers, from Weber's *Der Freischütz*, and the apprehensive Falstaff, disguised as Herne the Hunter, hearing the chimes of midnight in Windsor Forest (Verdi's *Falstaff*, final scene).

SOME NEW TIME-PATTERNS

We have learnt how to divide a crotchet beat into halves, called quavers. We can now think about quarter-beats, called semiquavers. To write a single semiquaver, worth a quarter of a crotchet beat, we simply add an extra tail to the quaver sign:

Four semiquavers, making up a whole crotchet, can have their tails fastened together:

Here is a rhythm-game to be played in three groups, A, B and C:

(Pupil's 45)

Group A   Clap quietly, steadily, and not too fast:

Group B   Tap with a finger on the palm of the other hand:

Group C   Tap like Group B, but twice as fast:

It is a good idea for Groups A and B to practise together first, and then for C to join in with the semiquavers. It will help Group C if they whisper the word *se-mi-qua-vers* while they tap.

Sometimes a crotchet has to be split into a half and two quarters, or two quarters and a half:

Group A Clap crotchets

Group B Tap quavers

Group C Tap and whisper *half-quar-ters*

When this has worked out right, try it the other way round:

quar-ters-half

(Pupil's 46)

There is one more pattern worth practising, because it comes so often in lively tunes. This pattern is made up of three quarters plus one quarter:

Group A Tap semiquavers

Group B Tap 'half-quar-ters'

Group C The same as Group B, but only *think* the first of the quarters

Group C's pattern is a jumpy rhythm that we usually write like this:

THE JOLLY MILLER

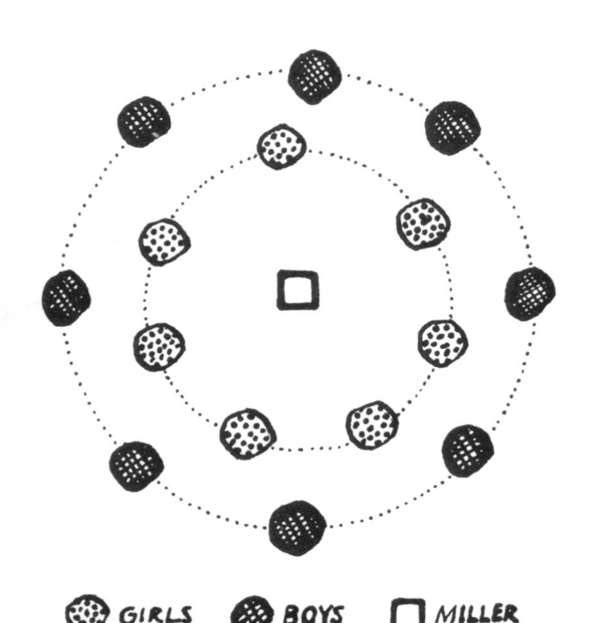

We have printed this in the A scale. As you can see, it contains semiquaver patterns. Make up your own percussion accompaniments, using drum, tambourines, cymbals, triangles and any other suitable instruments. Choose any of the time-patterns marked 'accompaniment', or have several of them going at the same time.

'The Jolly Miller' used to be a favourite play-song or party game. An outer circle of boys and an inner circle of girls (one fewer than the number of boys) formed the 'wheel'. The 'miller', stood in the middle of the wheel. The two circles walked round in opposite directions. At the word 'grab' every boy including the 'miller', tried to catch a partner, and the one left without any had to take his turn as the 'miller'.

(Pupil's 47)

There was a jol-ly mil-ler and he lived by him-self, As the

wheel went round he made his wealth; One hand on the hopper and the

other in the bag, As the wheel went round he made his grab.

Accompaniment:

(etc.)

(Pupil's 48)

DAY DAWNS WITH FREIGHT TO HAUL

This is a dock-workers' song from East Africa, very short but sung over and over again while loading or unloading cargo. The hauling shouts of *e-ya* should be pronounced '*ay-yah*'.

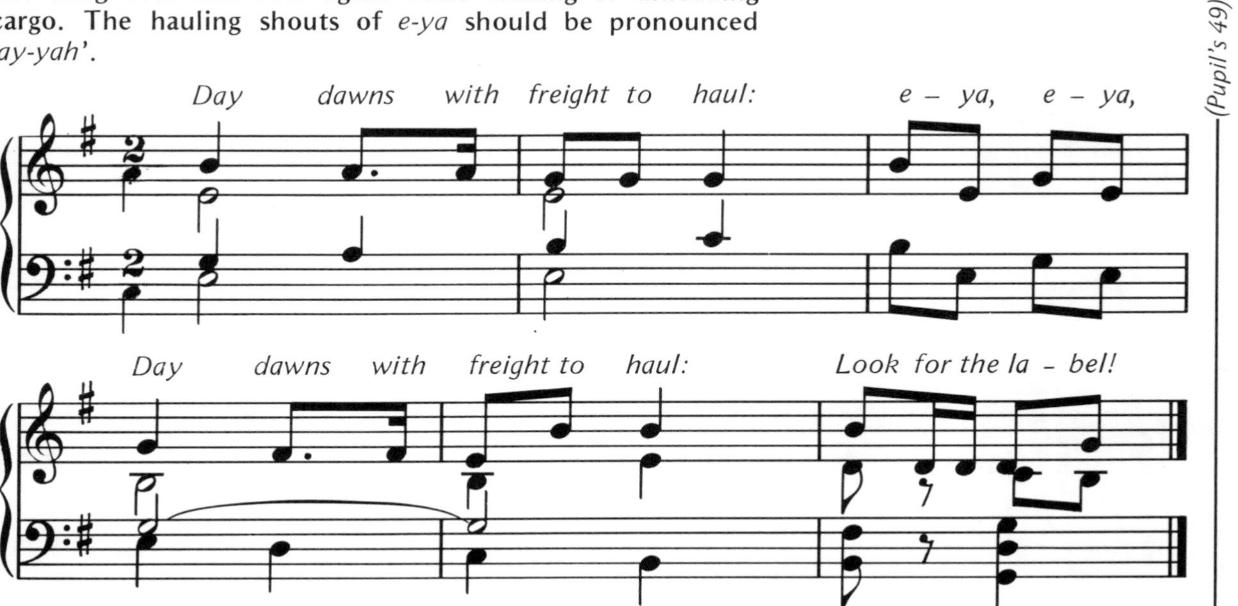

(Pupil's 49)

TALL STORIES

This comes from Spain, where no one is expected to take the words seriously:

(Pupil's 50)

(1) rab – bits in a tree were bea – ting on a drum.
(2) field – mouse I saw cha – sing an old cat called Tom.
(3) chic – kens and a vix – en in a friend – ly talk.
[After verse 3]:
O no? O yes! But a - ny-way, I vow My
stock of these tall sto - ries is all fi – nished now.
(Pupil's 50)

Things to do

1 Practise writing semiquavers:

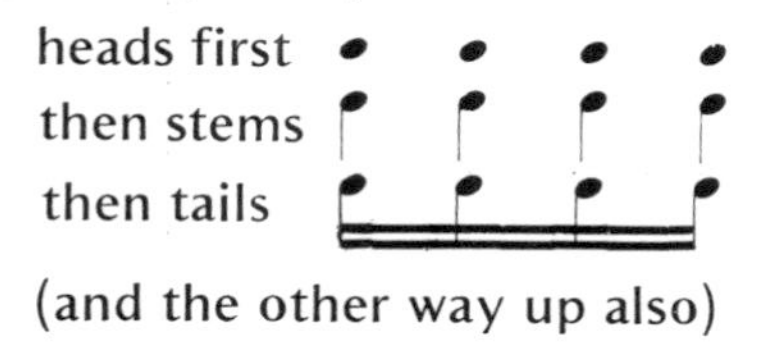

(and the other way up also)

2 Collect more songs with nonsense words, such as 'The Derby Ram' and 'The Crocodile'.

3 Play this old Welsh tune on the recorder, and write out percussion parts to go with it, remembering that it is a march. It is played and sung both in Wales and across the sea in Brittany. Just as many Welsh people speak two languages, Welsh and English, so many of the Bretons speak Breton, which sounds something like Welsh, as well as French.

There is a story that long ago in a war between Britain and France, soldiers from Wales and Brittany found themselves on opposite sides. But when each army heard the other singing the same marching-song, and orders being shouted in nearly the same words, they refused to fight and shook hands.

(Pupil's 51/52)

CAPTAIN MORGAN'S MARCH

(The sets of dots between the spaces of the stave are *repeat signs*, and mean that each pair of phrases should be played twice.)

TEACHING NOTES

1 The semiquaver groupings are easier than they look, except for the dotted-quaver-semiquaver figure which constantly occurs and is the most useful of all. Group practice along the lines suggested should soon make it familiar and secure. The groups can of course be switched round so that all have a turn with the harder groupings.

2 'The Jolly Miller', once widely known from home and school parties, is now probably forgotten except by the older generation. It is unlikely that teenagers will be drawn to reviving it as a game, but the tune is good enough to form the basis for percussion improvisation and scoremaking, in itself quite an absorbing exercise.

3 The East African work song is taken by permission from *Songs and Tales from the Dark Continent* by Natalie Curtis, and appears in the *Botsford Collection of Folk Songs*, Volume 1, published by Schirmer. It is best sung without accompaniment.

4 The Spanish nonsense song *Embustes* has been freely translated from *Cancionero musical español*, edited by Eduardo M. Torner and published by Harrap & Co. Ltd.

English nonsense songs like 'The Derby Ram', 'The Crocodile', and 'The Great Meat Pie' can be found in many books of traditional and folk songs. This might also be an opportunity to introduce some of Kodály's music to *Háry Jańos*, a play about a richly mendacious old Hungarian soldier (the Prelude starts with a sneeze, traditionally a warning that what follows is to be taken with a grain of salt).

5 *Captain Morgan's March* is a traditional Welsh harp tune. In Brittany the same melody is called *The Siege of Guingamp*. Several English versions of the words have been printed, but are generally difficult to sing, being full of Victorian poetic diction and historical allusions, so that the instrumental treatment suggested here may be preferred.

WINDMILLS AND WATERMILLS

Every kind of food-grain – wheat, barley, oats, maize, rye and millet – has to be ground or pounded into meal or flour before it can be baked or prepared in some other way for eating. In some parts of the world handmills are still used; they consist of a flat or hollowed-out lower stone and a heavy upper stone with which to rub or beat the grain. The upper stone often has one or two handles fixed to it so that two people, sitting each side of the mill, can share the labour of turning it. A handmill of this kind is sometimes called a quern. Handmilling was a long wearisome job, and it was generally the women who were expected to do it. To make it go a little more easily they sang as they turned. Here is an old Irish quern song with a pentatonic tune:

(Pupil's 53)

THE QUERN TUNE

Words by A. P. Graves

Down in a shower falls the flour.
Win - ding strong, grind-ing all day long, Round, round and
round goes the mill; Grind-ing turn a-bout, till the meal is out, must
ne-ver, ne - ver stand still.

It was probably in eastern lands that men discovered how to use the powers of wind and water to turn huge circular stones and grind enough grain to feed whole villages. Windmills were being used in Arab countries at least a thousand years ago, and in time they were introduced into Greece, Spain, France, and other parts of Europe. Many were built in the eastern counties of England and in the lowlands of Holland, where they were made not only to grind corn but also to pump water out of marshy land.

Watermills too seem to have been invented in the Arab countries. They work by having a strong stream of water pouring on to wooden blades fixed to a large wheel, which is connected to machinery for turning the grinding-stones inside the mill-house. Tide-mills are similar, but are built near river estuaries in order to harness the power of the tides as they ebb and flow. There were at least five thousand water-mills and tide-mills in England by the year 1086, when they were listed in William the Conqueror's Domesday Book. Water continued to be the main source of power for factories (still called 'mills' in northern England) until the invention of the steam engine.

In the Isle of Man there is a glen where a water-mill can still be seen, though it no longer grinds corn. This song was made about it when it was still working:

(Pupil's 54/55)

MANX GRINDING SONG

English version by Mona Douglas

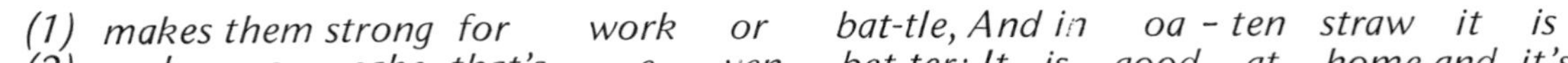

(1) makes them strong for work or bat-tle, And in oa - ten straw it is
(2) make a cake that's e - ven bet-ter; It is good at home and it's
(3) that a__ lone I'll take my portion, It will give new life to the

(1) good to lie; O the mill, the mill O, And the corn crop that is new, And the
(2) good for church; O the mill, the mill O, And the corn crop that is new, And the
(3) sick at heart; O the mill, the mill O, And the corn crop that is new, And the

(1) lit-tle grains of oats are go - ing to the mil - ler. ________
(2) lit-tle grains of wheat are go - ing to the mil - ler. ________
(3) lit-tle grains of bar - ley go - ing to the mil - ler. ________

The miller used to be one of the most important men in the village, and one of the most prosperous, as his work was useful to everybody. This explains why there are so many songs about him. Some of them describe how he was paid by 'taking toll' — that is, keeping an agreed share of the flour from each customer for his own use; not always fairly, perhaps, but other tradesmen did the same, if we can believe this French song:

WHEN THE MILLER STARTS A-MILLING

(Pupil's 55/56)

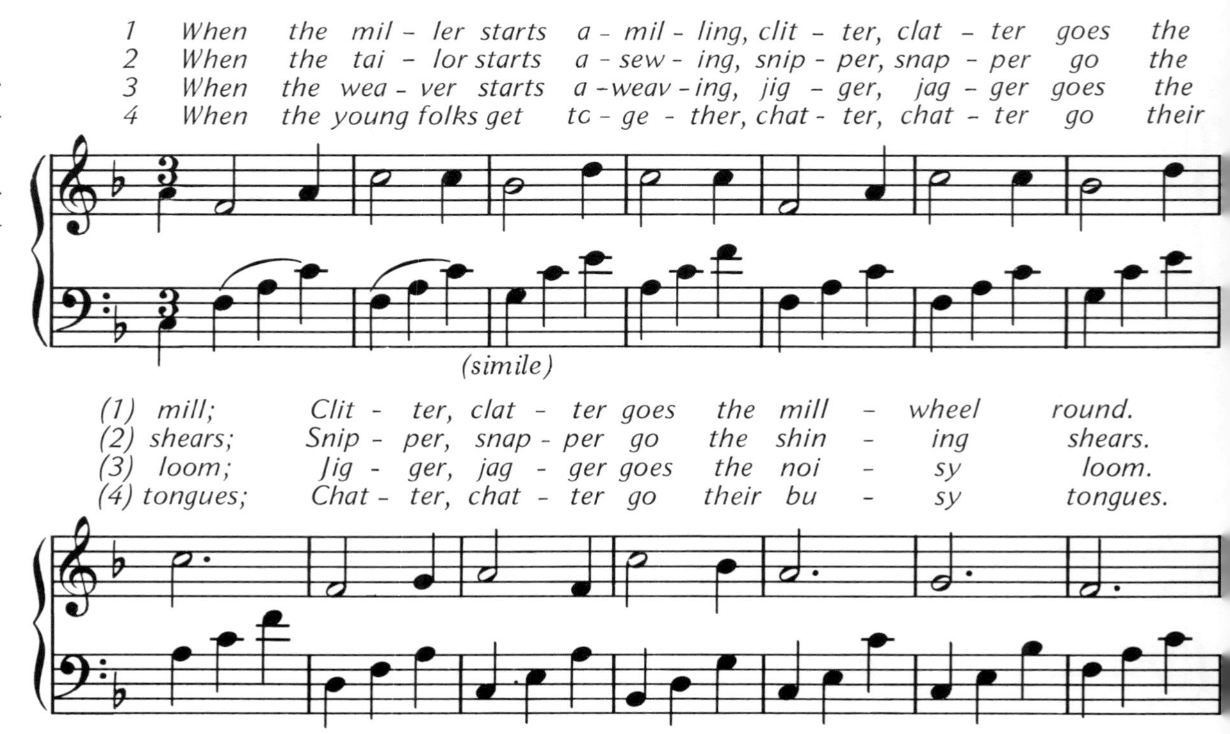

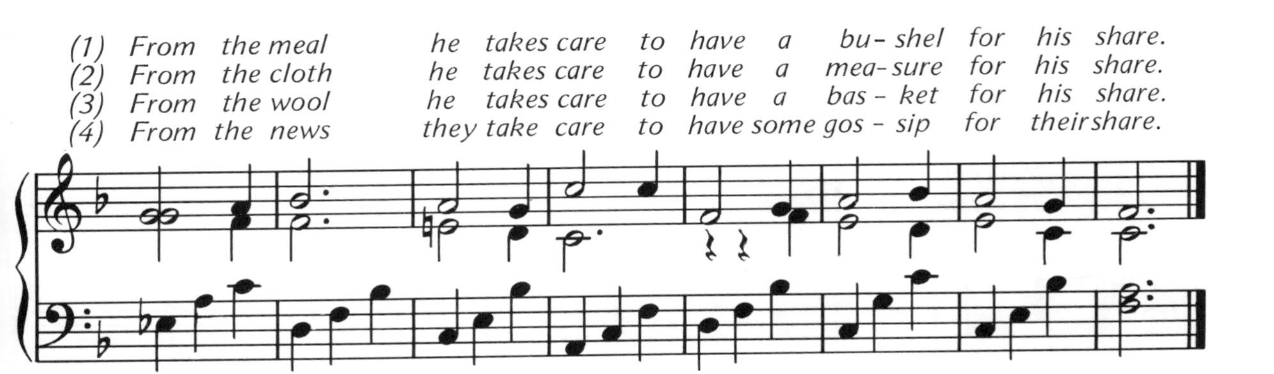

Another thing that was sometimes said about the miller was that he had a problem finding a suitable wife. An English song and a Dutch one both mention this point. To understand the Dutch song, remember that the sails of a windmill have to be set to catch the wind from whatever direction it happens to be blowing. In England this was usually managed by means of an ingenious 'fantail' wheel, invented in 1745 by a miller named Edmund Lee. The fantail catches any wind and turns the cap or top of the mill, sails and all, in the right direction. In Holland the sails had to be pulled round with a pole fixed to the cap, a chore that might account for the trouble the Dutch miller had in making up his mind.

(Pupil's 57)

THERE WAS A MAID WENT TO THE MILL

(Pupil's 58)

WHEN THE WIND COMES FROM THE SOUTHERN SIDE

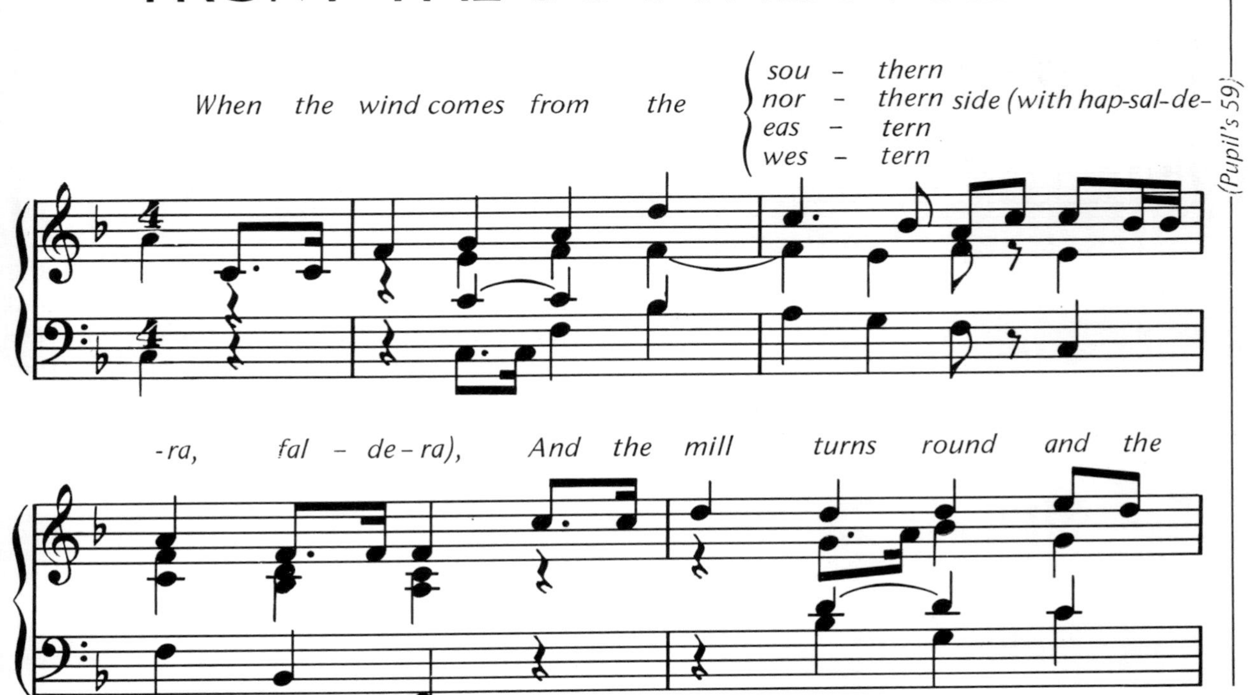

(Pupil's 60)

The sound of the machinery, with the chugging of the big water-wheel, has found its way into many mill songs. Here are two: the first, which is very short, is from Czechoslovakia, and the second tells of a contented life in a French mill:

(Pupil's 60)

CZECH MILL SONG

HARK TO THE MILL-WHEELS

(Pupil's 61)

Things to do

(Pupil's 63)

1 Find out if there are any windmills or watermills (working or not) in your district, and look out for more when you go on holiday. A large-scale map usually marks them. Some old windmills have been restored and can be visited. There is plenty to learn about the various kinds of windmill – 'tower', 'post', and 'smock', and about the different kinds of sails. Watermills too have different ways of using the water, as the wheels may be 'overshot' or 'undershot'. If you are interested in machinery, you can find out how wind or water power is made to turn the millstones through systems of gears. Then you can go on to find out how milling is done nowadays without the old sources of power (though the principle of the watermill is used in the turbine for generating electricity).

2 Look for more songs about millers, like 'The miller of the Dee', and a North Country ballad, 'The miller and his three sons' which is about toll-taking.

(Pupil's 62)

3 The picture on page 76 shows some watermills in Germany several hundreds of years ago. The mill closest to us has been built beside a river, from which water is forced through a narrow opening (notice the little waves) and turns two mill-wheels under the archways. The water-wheels are made of wood, and wooden gears fit into one another and drive round the mill-stones in the room above. Look carefully at the picture and you will see that:

(a) Each pair of mill-stones is supplied with grain through a kind of trough or hopper.
(b) Horses or mules loaded with sacks of grain are arriving at the mill.
(c) The miller is weighing sacks of grain, while another man (in the window) seems to be writing down the weights in a book. The weighing machine is of the kind called a 'steelyard'.
(d) Two of the miller's men are pouring grain into the hoppers. There is also a boy; can you guess what his job is?
(e) A spare mill-stone, with its grooves, is leaning against the wall outside.
(f) Chickens, ducks or geese, and pigeons belong to the mill. Why are these profitable for the miller to keep?
(g) In the distance are two floating mills, looking like Noah's arks. Why do you think they are kept near the middle of the river? How are they connected to the river bank?

(Pupil's 63/64)

TEACHING NOTES

1 More songs have been included than will be needed by any single class or group, and there is a large amount of background material.

2 'The Quern Tune' is not at all easy to sing to the words written by A. P. Graves: his complete version printed in *The National Song Book* is even more elaborate. One solution is to hum the melody, or better still vocalise it (Swingle-wise). The French traditional 'Quand le meunier s'en va moudre' is translated by permission from Bernard Fuller's *La France qui chante*, where it is more rationally given in 6/8 notation; here 3/4 is used to avoid anticipating the material of a later section, but a good lively tempo is essential. The Manx 'Grinding Song' was collected from Margot Quale at Glen Aldyn Mill, and translated by Mona Douglas. The Dutch 'Molenaartjes wind is zuidenwind' is translated from *Nederlands Volkslied*, edited by Jop Pollman and Piet Tiggers.

3 Recommended for the class working library is **Windmills of East Anglia*, by Brian Flint, published by F. W. Pawsey & Sons, Ipswich, 1973. Though only a few pages long, this is packed with information and illustrated with beautiful colour photographs. The still smaller **I Spy in the Country* is also helpful about windmills. A larger book, but quite easy to come by, is *The Shell Book of Country Crafts*, which goes into details of machinery. Recommended also are the booklets, *Discovering Windmills* and *Discovering Watermills*, by John Vince (*Shire Publications*, Princes Risborough).

A fascinating book for the teacher, and to some extent for pupils also, is *Windmills and Watermills* by John Reynolds (published by Hugh Evelyn, London, 1970). While profusely illustrated and authoritatively detailed, it is also superbly written. The author's enthusiasm for aesthetic as well as technical aspects of his subject communicates itself to the least mechanically-minded reader, and the finely-produced photographs and engravings make the book a joy to handle.

4 The song (derived from an English folk tune) 'The Miller of the Dee' can be found in *The National Song Book* and other collections. 'The Miller and his Three Sons' is printed in *North Countrie Folk Songs*, edited by W. G. Whittaker.

The following are among the many relevant works available in recordings:

(a) François Couperin: *Les petits moulins à vent*, a harpsichord piece that might be within the capacity of a Grade 5 or 6 pianist.

(b) Richard Strauss: *Don Quixote* (the exciting episode where the Don attacks a row of windmills, believing them to be giants).

(c) Ralph Vaughan Williams: *The Water-Mill*, an evocative setting of a poem by Fredegond Shove.

(d) Franz Schubert: *Die schöne Müllerin*, inspired from beginning to end with the sounds and life of a romantic watermill.

KING BRAMBLE

Once upon a time all the trees agreed to choose one of themselves and anoint him as their king.
First they said to the olive tree:

Come and reign over us.

But the olive tree replied:
'Why should I give up my rich oil, which is used for honouring God and man, in order to become chief of all the trees?'
Then they said to the fig tree:

Come and reign over us.

But the fig tree replied:
'Why should I give up my sweetness and my good fruit, and become chief among the trees?'
Then the trees said to the vine:

Come and reign over us.

And the vine answered them:
'Why should I leave my grapes, which give wine for God and man, in order to become chief among the trees?'
Then last of all the trees called to the bramble:

Come and reign over us.

And the bramble answered the trees:
'If you really want me as your king, you can come and put your trust in my shadow. But remember that fire can leap out of the bramble, fierce enough to devour the cedars of Lebanon, which are the greatest of all the trees.'

(Pupil's 65)

Things to do

1 This story is taken from the Book of Judges (Chapter 2) in the Old Testament of the Bible. Try to make a series of pictures to illustrate it. They can be coloured or black and white drawings, or they can be pictures in sound.

2 Here are some ideas for sounds:

The trees agreeing to elect a king Heavy instruments, like large drums, can represent the trunks of the larger trees; lighter instruments, like small drums and rattles, their swaying branches; and delicate instruments, like tambourines and triangles, their rustling foliage. Find a rhythm-pattern for the words '*Come and reign over us*', and use it each time the words occur in the story.

The olive tree Find out all you can about the olive. Its fruit, which looks like green plums, contains oil used for cooking and salad. How can the oil 'honour God and man'? The answer is in the use of oil in religious ceremonies and at coronations. The olive tree is also prized for its beautifully grained wood. Choose instruments with a smooth, gentle sound for the olive (recorders might be suitable) and try letting them play in thirds, perhaps like this:

The fig tree One of the curious things about the fig is that it bears its fruit before the leaves open. What are the leaves like? What colour is the fruit when it first forms, and when it is ripe? The story mentions the sweetness of the fig, so find some sweet-toned instruments to represent it. Chime bars or glockenspiels might do, playing either in thirds, or better still in sixths to distinguish the fig from the olive:

(Pupil's 66)

The vine Everyone has seen bunches of green or purple grapes in shops, or even growing outdoors in warm and sheltered positions. Music for the vine should suggest the twisting slender stems of the plant, its delicate tendrils, and the hanging bunches of fruit. It might also suggest the lively scenes, with dancing, that take place in warm countries when the ripe grapes are being gathered and the wine pressed out. This will mean plenty of quaver or semiquaver time-patterns, including dotted notes, and rhythmic percussion as well as melodic instruments.

The bramble The bramble is able to grow in rough, dry ground and it protects its soft and juicy fruit with prickly thorns. Instruments with a dry, hard sound would therefore be best for the bramble's music: try wooden instruments such as xylophones (played with hard-headed sticks), wood blocks, claves, castanets, and guiros (scrapers). The sound-picture should be full of irregular, jagged noises, and should represent not only the bramble itself but also the fire it threatens. It might make a good ending to the whole piece if all the other trees could join in with their own music, while the bramble sounds try to swallow them up.

(Pupil's 67)

Fitting words and sound-pictures together The words of the story can be shared among many voices, all speaking together or separately for the replies of the different trees. The speakers can stop and wait for the sound-pictures to be played, and then go on to the next part of the story. With some practice, the musicians can learn to start just before the speaking voices have finished their sentences, so that the whole story unrolls itself in words and music.

If you are interested in dancing, you could work out a ballet of group and solo dances to illustrate the story.

TEACHING NOTES

1 This is an elaborate creative project, involving the use of any sound-resources available to the pupils, and backed by factual research in several fields.
2 It offers scope for co-operation with other departments — religious education, speech and drama, geography, biology, literature, and the other arts.
3 Tape-recording would be a helpful method of trying out various sound-effects and of putting the whole structure together in its completed form.
4 The story is an Old Testament parable, from *Judges* 2, verses 8-15. The Authorised Version can of course be used instead of the modernised paraphrase given in the pupils' books. A reference book like *Helps to the Study of the Bible* can be consulted for details of the trees mentioned.

MORE ABOUT SCALES

By now we are quite used to the scale pattern that has the eight singing names:

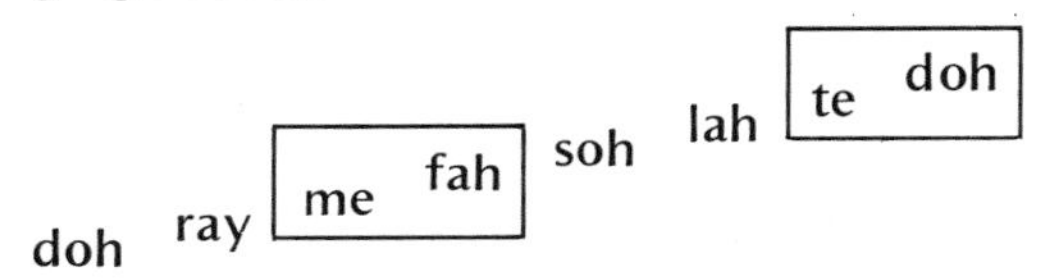

We can always recognise this pattern when we hear it, because of the two semitone steps between *me-fah* and *te-doh*. It does not matter what note we choose for *doh*; the scale will sound right as long as the tones and semitones come in the same order. We have already used these notes as *doh*:

C

G (needing an F sharp for *te*)

D (needing an F sharp for *me* and a C sharp for *te*)

A (needing an F sharp for *lah*, a C sharp for *me*, and a G sharp for *te*)

F (needing a B flat for *fah*)

Now let us add two more scales to the list.
Suppose we try to build a scale with the usual pattern, starting from B flat. We shall soon find that we need an extra flat to make the *me-fah* semitone:

(We start from a low B flat, to make a scale that is comfortable to sing.) The new note is E flat.

(Pupil's 68)

Now take this E flat and make it the starting-note; once more we shall have to use a new note, A flat, for the *me-fah* semitone:

To avoid writing these flats each time we need them, we put them as key signatures at the beginning of a piece of music:

(Pupil's 69)

Rules to learn

If there is no key signature, *doh* is C

If there is a sharp key signature, the sharp furthest to the right is *te*

If there is a flat key signature, the flat furthest to the right is *fah*

Major and minor

Most of the tunes we have sung and played up to now finish with *doh*. We say they are in the *major mode*.

But many tunes finish with *lah*, like this song from Russia:

THE BIRCH TREE

These *lah* tunes are in a *minor mode*. They usually (though not always) have a sadder sound than the major-mode tunes. Here is a round, printed with the key signature of one flat which shows that F is *doh* and D is *lah*. There is also an extra sharp (C sharp) to make a semitone step up to *lah*. When this happens we give it a special singing name, *se*:

AH POOR BIRD

The round can be sung by two, three, or four groups of voices, each starting the tune when the previous group has finished the first bar (that is, the first three words). Each group should sing the whole tune three times and then drop out.

Minor-mode tunes are not all sad. Here is a very jolly one, from the days before tractors and lorries, when all the farm work had to be carried on by the strength of men and horses. For the heaviest jobs a team of horses was used, and the carter was responsible for looking after the animals and making them understand what to do. Some of the carter's shouts to the horses come near the end of the song. '*Hey*' means 'turn right', '*hee*' means 'turn left', '*hoo*' is 'stop', and '*gee*' is 'go on'. This was sometimes used as a forfeit song when work was over for the day and everyone was looking for some amusement. Four different people would then try to give the right shout at the right time, and the one who missed would have to pay for drinks for the others.

'Bears the bell' means 'is the best of the team'.

(Pupil's 70/71)

THE CARTER'S HEALTH

Hey, there is Ree, there is Hoo, there is Gee, but the bob-tailed mare bears the
bell a - way. There is Hey, there is Ree, there is Hoo, there is Gee, but the
bob-tailed mare bears the bell a - way. Hey, Ree,
Hoo, Gee, but the bob-tailed mare bears the bell a - way.

Things to do

1 Here is a Breton dance tune, arranged for two players. The tune is in the top line, while the lower line has an accompaniment that moves up and down the steps of the minor scale. *Doh* is G, and *lah* (on which the tune begins and ends) is E:

(Pupil's 73)

2 These are the beginnings of five major-mode tunes. All are national anthems. Decide what keys they are in, sing or play them, and find what countries they belong to:

(Pupil's 74)

3 These are the beginnings of three well-known minor tunes. See if you can recognise them, and then try to play them right through:

TEACHING NOTES

1 By adding two more flat keys (B flat and E flat majors), this section completes the range of key-signatures to be learnt in the course. With the 'open' key of C major and three sharp and three flat major keys, and their relative minors, the average young musician will have a working knowledge adequate for most practical purposes. In fact string and wind players will seldom need more, while keyboard players can extend their key-geography without undue difficulty if they are fluent in the first seven keys.

2 Trying to put off indefinitely any reference to the minor mode and its notation is liable to produce dull uniformity in both melody and harmony, since so much music — classical, folk, and pop — is minor in tonality. On the other hand, detailed study of the forms of minor scale is out of place in general class music at this stage. The minor mode is less consistent in pattern, and correspondingly more complex in notation, than the major. But its flexibility is high among the qualities that make it so valuable and attractive a resource, and we cannot afford to neglect it in elementary teaching.

This section therefore aims at giving some enjoyable examples of minor melodies and developing some sense of their differences, aural and structural, as compared with major tunes. As far as notation goes, the minor scales are linked with the more common major keys, but without attempting to classify the various types of minor scale, or even to discuss why we use the particular terms 'major' and 'minor'.

Whereas we have to deal with only one form of major, the minor mode occurs in at least three, and more than one may occur in the same brief melody. The only variable note introduced in this course is the seventh step of the scale, which may either be the modal *soh* or the semitonal 'leading-note' *se*. It seems best for the present to treat the latter as an accidental in notation (sharp or natural, and liable to be cancelled), rather than to go into the whole question of how far it is a regular feature of the minor scale or why it is not included in key signatures.

3 The teaching procedures adopted here depend in the first place on full acceptance of the *lah*-minor principle. This is not the place to present all the arguments against *doh*-minor, except to remark that the latter rests on shaky historical and logical foundations, and makes nonsense of any attempt to apply it to modal melodies. Given this assumption, we distinguish three patterns of minor, though we do not need to pass the scheme on to the elementary non-specialist pupil:

(a) lah [te doh] ray [me fah] soh lah	(the so-called Aeolian mode, the familiar semitones, in reverse order)
(b) lah te doh ray [me fah] [se lah]	('harmonic minor', with three semitones)
(c) lah [te doh] ray me bay [se lah]	('ascending melodic minor' with two semitones, and a raised 6th step)

We disregard (c) in this course, and as far as (a) and (b) are concerned there is no difference except that the last step is sometimes *soh-lah*, sometimes *se-lah*. If possible, a few short tunes should be learnt by heart with sol-fa syllables (singing names): for example, 'The birch tree', which is modal, and 'Ah poor bird' which has the sharpened leading note.

4 The tune-openings for recognition under *Things to do* will help to strengthen the links between tonality and notation.* The E natural in 1(a) can be regarded as a chromatic note, without troubling at this stage about a possible modulation. Both 3(a) and 3(b) are sometimes found in other forms of minor; here they are quoted in modal versions. Abler pupils can be encouraged not only to try to sing or play the melodies complete, but also to write them out.

5 From this point onward, melodic material may be given in any of the specified seven major keys or their relative minors.

*The solutions are (major-mode) (a) *The Star-spangled banner*, (b) *Land of my fathers*, (c) *Austria* ("Glorious things of thee are spoken"), (d) *O Canada*, (e) *La Marseillaise*.
(minor-mode): (a) *Greensleeves*, (b) *God rest you merry, gentlemen*, (c) *What shall we do with a drunken sailor*?